Search for the Pearl

Inside Yourself

A Gift of Encouragement

For a Special Young Adult

Written and Compiled by

Diana Jackson

Search for the Pearl

Inside Yourself

A Gift of Encouragement

For a Special Young Adult

Written and Compiled

by

Diana Jackson

ISBN 978-1-8381526-0-4

All photos were taken on the island of Alderney by the author.

Published in Great Britain in 2021 by Eventispress

Printed by Biddles Books Ltd, Norfolk

Dedicated

To all of the students who have given

me such pleasure over the years of a

lifetime teaching. Many thanks

Diana

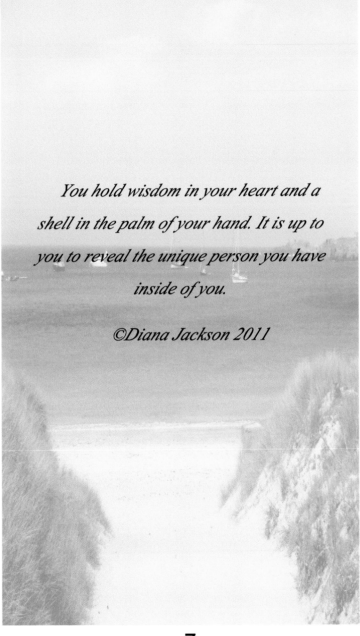

You hold wisdom in your heart and a shell in the palm of your hand. It is up to you to reveal the unique person you have inside of you.

©Diana Jackson 2011

Foreword

One day I picked up a copy of 'Chicken Soup for the Soul'. I flicked through the pages and was drawn to the story of a teacher who, at the end of the year, called a few of his pupils into his office. He gave out certificates but to one he gave a small box and in it was a tiny pearl.

The message of the story was so simple that it made me think of all the young people I have wished to encourage over the years. I could see their potential; I believed that the future would be successful for them, but they just needed to believe in themselves.

Pearls are as Special as You Are

Shapes of pearls include round, drop, oval, button, semi-round & baroque. There are black pearls, white, grey, pink and cream.

Just like people, all natural pearls are unique.

Pearls are valued by their individual qualities - size, shape, lustre, blemishes or lack of them. There's no 'better' or 'worse' pearl - the simplicity of each pearl is its beauty.

A Gift for You

Someone who believes in you has given you this small book. It may be from a special friend, parent, aunt or uncle or it may be from a teacher, tutor or employer. Certainly, it is from someone who feels that you need encouragement to realise your true potential.

~ Believe you me, they can already see the glimmer of what you might become, shining from deep within you.

Did you know that every pearl begins as a bit of grit or fragment of shell? To relieve the irritation to the oyster, the creature covers it, layer upon layer, which eventually forms a beautiful pearl.

At first you may just flick through the pages and toss 'Search for the Pearl...' up on to a dusty high shelf, out of reach and out of mind.

This book may even find a place of honour on your bedside table.

Either way, I hope that its presence may continue to irritate your sub conscious being, in the same way that the memory sometimes searches for a forgotten name or an answer to a question which has just slipped the mind.

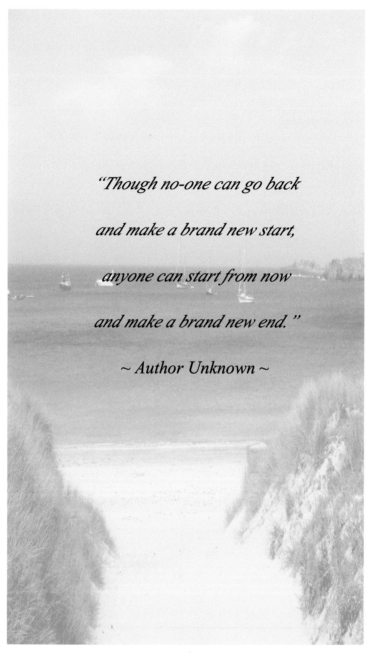

"Though no-one can go back

and make a brand new start,

anyone can start from now

and make a brand new end."

~ Author Unknown ~

Let go of the Past

Your path of understanding can begin by being honest about who you are at this moment in time.

Why are you feeling uncertain or filled with doubt? Is it something a person has said to you? Is it something you have done or not done?

It is important, however insignificant or massive these thoughts might be, that you acknowledge your part in them, take responsibility for yourself, then let those feelings and thoughts go. In this lies the way to freedom from their hold on you. Here's how you can

let go and move on:

There are many ways to set yourself free. You need to find the right way for you.

If your faith is your strength, calling upon your higher power could be the perfect way.

You could go for a stroll on an stormy day and imagine your thoughts being blown away by the wind ...

or by a raging river or sea, to be lost in the depths of the ocean.

It might help to write down those thoughts; memories which are troubling you and stealing your peace. Once written, tear them up into very small pieces. Then you could set fire to the paper ~ or dig a hole and place your writing deep down, letting them be decomposed naturally into earth.

Air Water Fire   Earth

Feel their cleansing and healing power.

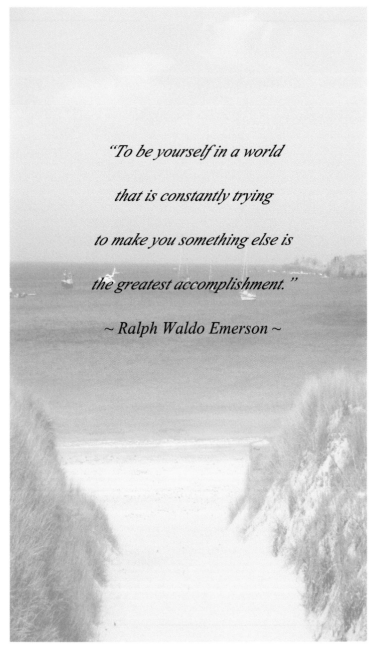

"To be yourself in a world

that is constantly trying

to make you something else is

the greatest accomplishment."

~ Ralph Waldo Emerson ~

Follow Your Instincts

You might also remember moments when you have searched for a way forward and have stumbled and felt lost for a while. Next you have found the courage and trusted to take the next step.

The stones in your path have miraculously disappeared, as you have instinctively followed the right route with no knowledge of the consequences.

Still your mind, listen carefully to your heart and head and follow your instincts.

Think of Your Achievements

Think of your life's achievements - the ones which spring to our mind might be learning to drive, passing exams, gaining employment or a place at college, but there are many others of equal importance:

It could be creating music, a work of art or being a great defender in football ~ a team player. You might be proud of learning to bake a cake, writing a song, mending a bicycle, fixing a problem with the PC or having patience and love to play with a younger sibling or family pet. We often ignore these accomplishments and take them for granted.

Celebrate success, both great and small

As you think of your successes in life, however large or small, dwell on these memories for a while.

You could write down a list or surround yourself with objects, pictures and photographs; anything to remind you of the good things you have done, places you have visited and people who have touched your life in a positive way; or maybe, unwittingly, you have made their lives more complete by being you.

~ How would you describe yourself?

What are your qualities?

(Kind, patient, a good friend, adventurous, quiet, thoughtful, determined ...)

~ What Skills do you have?

IT, creative writing, design, mechanical aptitude ... are the obvious type of skills

(Are you good at talking to others or at design? Do you knit, cook, map read or take great photos. Don't forget if sport is your passion, participating rather than watching! You may care for animals or the environment, be a climber or sooth a baby to sleep with ease...)

~ Do you have any academic achievements?

Although listing qualifications are the most obvious here, don't worry if you have none or only a few. Did you have a favourite class at school, PE or art for example? (I put my swimming certificates on my first CV~ I was so proud to have swum a mile!)

"The future belongs to those

who believe in

the beauty of

their dreams."

Eleanor Rooselvelt

What do you need to change?

Now is the time to think about change. Which parts of your life do you think should remain as a firm foundation for your future?

Which facets of your life have loose footings and need restoration or even rebuilding and which parts need knocking down altogether?

It may be that you need to learn a new skill, enrol on a course or refresh a pastime you have recently neglected.

It may be that you have a gift or talent which has lain dormant and needs reawakening.

"When the winds of change blow,

some people build walls

and others build windmills."

Chinese Proverb

Begin to Dream

What would your perfect life look like? Close your eyes and try to imagine it. How would it be possible to reach this fantasy world you are dreaming about and how can you make it a reality?

If thinking about this is too difficult, let's break it down into smaller steps.

Now is the time to think of your goals and visions of the future. As you answer the questions on the next few pages, your reply may be

'I am happy as I am.'

If you are content in one area of your life described, or even uncertain at present, move on to the next question. Take a pause between each page and allow your subconscious mind to work its magic.

Who would you like to be with?

Family, friends, someone special - sometimes in life it feels like we have no choice, because decisions to be together work both ways, or we may have lost someone very close.

But we do have choices – learn to make positive ones about who you spend your time with. Try to spend time with those who enrich your life or you feel you enrich theirs.

Be wary of negative influencers on your life who can drain your sense of well being and self worth.

Some people come into our lives for a particular moment in time and some remain close forever. Learn to make the effort to keep in touch but also, in some cases, to let go.

Where would you truly like to be?

By the sea,

in a city,

in a foreign country,

in a village,

somewhere quiet and isolated,

somewhere busy and neighbourly.

If you are not sure, then think of places where you have felt happiest.

You may have no choice. If the answer to this is 'yes', is there any way you can change the space you are now in to find a greater sense of self worth?

Don't forget, there's no harm in having aspirations for the future.

35

"It's the action, not the fruit of the action, that's important. You have to do the right thing. It may not be in your power, may not be in your time, that there'll be any fruit. But that doesn't mean you stop doing the right thing. You may never know what results come from your action. But if you do nothing then there will be no result."

Ghandi

What would you like to do?

You may not know as yet, but try to be aware of clues around you, something you might read, a passing conversation or even something on the television. It may be that a thought just appears in your head and it feels just right.

Be open and listen;

trust in your instincts.

If you try something and it doesn't work, or the way is blocked somehow, look back through your journey with this little book and see if another way springs to mind. You will become stronger if you don't give up. You're worth it!

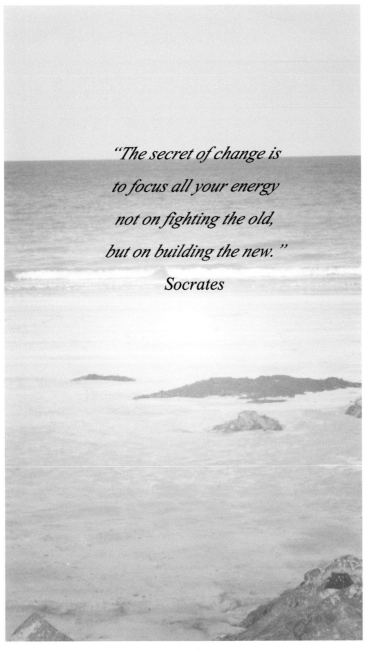

*"The secret of change is
to focus all your energy
not on fighting the old,
but on building the new."*

Socrates

"When one door closes, another opens:

But we often look so long and so regretfully upon the closed door

That we do not see the one which has opened for us."

Alexander Graham Bell

42

You are not alone

Don't be afraid to accept help along the way. Seek for opportunities and ask to be given a chance. Show your genuine desire to succeed.

Take set-backs as times when, temporarily, you tried the wrong turning; rest assured that there is another way forward. Believe in yourself.

In these uncertain times you may need to think differently. On-line courses, apprenticeships, the armed services where you can learn vital skills or even voluntary work, which could give you an excellent work ethic, a good reference and also achieve something worthwhile for the community. These are all ways forward, open to those who look.

Try to remain positive!

Find the Pearl Inside You

Take your time. Revisit pages of this book whenever you need encouragement.

Let the thoughts of this book continue to irritate, just as the piece of broken shell or grit irritates the oyster to produce a beautiful pearl.

You have the potential of a unique and stunning pearl growing inside you as you gain wisdom to make it happen.

Other Books by Diana Jackson

Motivational and Inspirational series:

The Healing Paths of Fife

Search for the Pearl Inside Yourself

Mystery Inspired by History series:

MURDER, Now and Then

MISSING, Past and Present

The Riduna series:

Riduna

Ancasta, Guide me Swiftly Home

Memoir:

The Life and Demise of Norman Campbell

The Healing Paths of Fife